Success Chests:
Mining Talent and Passion
to Fashion Success

Andrea J. Robles

Table of content

Dedication

This book is dedicated to every individual out there that refuse to give up despite their number of failures

Introduction

The old-age question of whether it is more important for one to have talent or for them to be more passionate about what they do has been on my mind a lot lately.

When you are building a team, is it more important to focus on how talented someone is? Can their abilities and range of skills propel them, and ultimately you, to the heights that you desire? Or is it better to have team members who are passionate about what they do? Can talent be a secondary factor in one's considerations?

In trying to answer this question, I think it is important to note that one cannot substitute for the other. One can be very passionate but if they do not have the talent to back the passion up, it becomes nearly impossible to execute tasks. If there is a talented individual who does not have any passion regarding what they do, it is difficult for them to be driven.

It is important to always try and find a balance between talent and passion. Both of these qualities are very important no matter what it is that you are trying to achieve.

Dwelling on this issue has made me conclude that when we are pairing clients and freelancers, it is important to make sure that the talent is placed in a field where they have some form of passion. It becomes easier for people to execute their duties when they are in a place where they believe they belong.

For far too long, people have been pursuing careers for what I believe are the wrong reasons. This has created a workforce that is not entirely happy with their jobs and as a result, they underperform when it comes to their duties. Let's find the right individuals for the right kind of jobs and we will have a workforce that is not only talented enough to achieve greatness but also passionate enough to want to see the greatness being achieved

Chapter 1

Two essential components of success are talent and passion. I had received several invitations to interviews for accounting positions within the last ten or so years, which I truly valued. Although most interview questions are predetermined, one question is consistently asked by interviewers:

"Why did you decide to switch from engineering to accounting?" The response to it is fairly straightforward: talent and passion. Although the idea of talent and passion may seem sensible and simple to grasp, many people decide not to pursue them for various reasons.

I will go into detail in this book on how using a talent and passion assessment in my decision-making process has opened up more (and better) commercial and professional opportunities for me. If your career is just getting started, you should give opportunities that match your enthusiasm and talent careful consideration. You will never work a day in your life if you do what you LOVE! Whoa! So you're persuaded that realizing the difference between talent and passion is essential to succeeding in the workplace or business?

But there are three basic things we need to know before we can apply this important life lesson. What do passion and talent mean? Why not follow your passion and talent? How can you find your passion and talent? What do passion and talent mean? Let's start by examining passion.

To put it simply, passion is the pursuit of something you love. In most cases, people have multiple areas of enthusiasm. Cooking, piano playing, and movie watching are possible passions. Another most likely enjoys reading, traveling, and playing the game of basketball. Passion is not something you are born with; it usually develops through life experiences. For instance, a person may become passionate about playing the piano after witnessing someone else do so and becoming genuinely interested in it. Saying that she was born with a strong desire to play the piano is just absurd. Talent is the second success aspect that we must comprehend.

Talent is more than just having a high level of performance; it's the ability to outperform others while putting up comparatively less effort. In contrast to enthusiasm, talent is innate and regrettably cannot be acquired via education or experience. Even if you have years of experience and become extremely excellent at something, it will still take you a lot longer to become an expert at it than it would for someone who is naturally gifted in that area.

Even though I lack scientific proof, I firmly think that everyone on the planet was born with at least one skill. It just requires searching for it, which is something that many people, regrettably, never manage to do throughout their lifetime. I quit engineering because of a lack of talent that ultimately led to a loss of enthusiasm. During my secondary and junior high school years, I had a strong interest in scientific and mathematics topics. As a "slightly more than average" science student, I ultimately chose to enroll in NTU's engineering program.

To my horrified astonishment, NTU had a sizable pool of gifted aspiring engineers. I devoted numerous hours to preparing for my first-year engineering exams, but my performance was well below expectations. My friends who were gifted engineers, on the other hand, studied for far less time and achieved unimaginable marks.

Since we were all living in the same residence hall, I could simply demonstrate that they weren't studying in secret. As I was frantically cramming for my tests in the early hours of the day, they were happily playing online games in their rooms with the door wide open. When you put in all of your work and yet can't succeed, it can be difficult to maintain your enthusiasm for the endeavor. I "gave up" on engineering after realizing I wasn't cut out for the field and started enrolling in business courses at Nanyang Business School instead of my required engineering courses. I was only formally pursuing an unofficial "double degree," so I didn't completely give up on engineering.

Although it was a hazardous wager, I knew that was not how life would continue. I had no idea about accounting, marketing, human resources, or finance. I did, however, adore them! My excitement increased as I read more about them. It was unexpectedly quick for me to comprehend what the writers were trying to convey!

Regretfully, nobody ever informed me that I needed to seek a career that was both something I was born to do and something I was enthusiastic about. I can relate to you if you are still in college or a polytechnic and are having difficulty with your studies because I have been there too. The best course of action, in my opinion, is for you to begin searching for your passion and talent and to focus all of your efforts on them. Ten years from now, you'll be tap dancing for work, as Warren Buffett puts it. Why not follow your passion and talent?

Hi there! If, ten years ago, I could not understand the advantages of matching my skill sets to my passion and talent, I would be insane to have wasted ten years of my life switching from engineering to business education. Although it took a while, the advantages are permanent.

Actually, despite the difficulties of working a full-time job and taking part-time ACCA classes, the anticipated benefits were what motivated me to continue.

The Top 3 advantages of following your passion and talent are listed here. If you are now going through a phase similar to what I went through a decade ago, hopefully, they will help you stay motivated.

Live a happier and more purposeful existence. Savor a higher caliber of life.

Lead a more fulfilling and happier life

I can still vividly remember the days when I was doing professional attachment at the end of the third year of my study in NTU Engineering. Due to the lack of talent in Engineering, I could only manage to secure a position in a local firm with around 5 employees – 2 of them were my schoolmates from NTU and the other one was myself.

By then, I had already been transitioning my skill sets to business and had also completely lost my passion for Engineering. It was a nightmare that lasted for 6 months. I hated what I was doing, dragging my feet to work, and was extremely demoralized all day long doing something that I completely was not interested in. Unfortunately, the sense of hopelessness did not end on Friday! The emotional torture continued through the weekend and hit its peak on Sunday evening to the point that it affected the people around me. While I knew it was only a professional attachment and it would be all over after 6 months, however, I told myself that this was not the kind of lifestyle I would want to lead for the next 40 or 50 years of my professional life!

I decided to escalate the intensity and accelerate the transition process to the business world.
More than a decade later, I jump out of my bed every morning looking forward to what I will be doing for the day. While I continue running several projects on the weekend, I do it at my own choice.

I have since stopped doing work that I am not passionate about and I am now leading a much more fulfilling and happier life.
The transition journey has not been an easy one, but if I can do it, you can do it too!

Without passion, you don't have energy.
Without energy, you have nothing.

Enjoy a better standard of living

Since the collapse of the Soviet Union in the early 1990s, it is probably clear that the capitalist economic system has prevailed. In a capitalist economic system, one of the ways to enhance our standard of living is through increasing our level of income.

Discovering and pursuing your talent and passion will ignite a chain of events that eventually allows you to raise your level of income. I have illustrated the chain of events through a simple diagram below.

Talent and Passion −> Positive Impression −> More Opportunities −> Higher Level of Income −> Enhanced Standard of Living

Let's see how this chain of events works in more detail.

Being passionate about what you are doing provides a certain level of comfort to recruiters, employers, and clients that you will be performing your tasks in the best possible manner. Being talented gives assurance to employers and clients that you will be able to solve their problems effectively and more efficiently as compared to the next guy. In combination, having both talent and passion creates a positive impression about you.

I had the privilege of working with 3 of the largest global recruitment firms (Robert Walters, Robert Half, and Michael Page) in my last 3 assignments. Having worked with them, I learned that being prominent recruitment firms, they can be quite influential to their clients – which is your employer-to-be!

It is therefore important that they do form a positive impression about you as they will in turn convince their clients that you are their top candidate for the position. In addition, I also learned that as long as I can create an initial positive impression with them, they will be more willing to share the opportunities that they have at hand.

Ability is nothing without opportunity.

Having more opportunities means that you have a higher chance to land yourself a position that provides a higher level of income, which in turn enhances your standard of living.

However, if you are still in the first decade of your professional life, I believe pursuing opportunities that provide you with the highest learning experience will be a wiser option.

Learning opportunities provide you with a better skill set which will then lead to a higher level of income, but unfortunately, the equation does not work the other way around. Position offering a higher level of income does not guarantee that you will be able to improve your skill set – which can prove to be quite risky in the future.

Build a wider social network

Whether your future aspiration is to climb the corporate ladder or build your own business, the importance of having a wide social network cannot be under-emphasized. Should you choose to progress in the corporate environment, there will be a point in time when you will have to lead a team in your chosen field.

You must start building a network of highly competent professionals so that one day you can consolidate them together as a single strong team. The significance of having a strong social network is self-explanatory if you decide to build your own business. You simply have no business if you do not know people and people do not know you. Nevertheless, thanks to Google, Facebook, and other digital marketing firms, building a business network has never been easier than ever before!

It is human nature that we enjoy being with people who are confident, optimistic and see their life as an exciting journey. Pursuing your talent and having passion for what you are doing will give you a purpose of existence in life and a sense of satisfaction which will in turn, motivate others to live their life to the fullest too.

While there is no doubt being passionate about professional or business life attracts like-minded individuals and expands your social network widely, it is also important to balance your network. I am personally still trying to find the secret formula that can allow me to balance my professional / business network and keep up with as many as personal friendships as possible.

How can you discover your talent and passion? Best wishes! You are committed to improving your quality of life if you have made it this far through the book. Finding your gift and passion should, in my opinion, be done as early as possible, preferably in your first ten years of professional life or while you are still enrolled in college or a polytechnic. It becomes more difficult for you to match your life with what it should be the longer you put off doing it.

So, how can you discover your talent and passion?

This question is probably best answered through sharing my own experience in discovering the amazing world of business – there is no other place I would rather be.

I am rolling up my sleeves as I try to begin writing this section. It is not going to be an easy journey, but it can be achieved and no words can describe the satisfaction when you finally accomplish it.

First and foremost, it's critical to acknowledge that people might be passionate about a variety of things. But most likely, each person only possesses one or, at most, a few abilities.

This is the reason you should start by looking for the things you are enthusiastic about while trying to identify your talent. In my case, I experimented with a lot of things that I liked to do when I was younger. I engaged in hoops. Even though I was consistently chosen for my school's squad, I was never able to reach the NBA. I picked up the piano. My piano teacher thought I had a lot of passion for the instrument, but she wasn't sure I would ever become the next Beethoven. I even made an effort to learn ballroom dancing! Obviously, with the lack of talent, I did not go very far. The list goes on.

As you can see, I experimented a lot before realizing my interest in business. In actuality, it took me nearly 25 years to find it. You should try out as many hobbies as you can if you're serious about finding something where your passion and talent match.

One of the things you are enthusiastic about is probably where your talent lies. This post takes a lot of late nights to write and publish. If you haven't been tap dancing to work every day, I genuinely hope that this post will inspire and advise you on how to eventually pursue a more fulfilling career and personal life.

Chapter 2

Finding Your Talent

There are times in our lives when we experience dejection and hopelessness. If no one else is around to boost our spirits, things get worse. In these situations, you must keep in mind that you are endowed with great talents and that you will be able to take control of your life once more once you realize this.

The hardest thing to answer, though, is how to recognize your talents. We are so busy with life's daily grind that we frequently neglect to take a step back and examine who we are. However, you begin to lose confidence when life knocks you to your knees. In these moments, you have to find your inner strength and courage.

You can identify your talent in several ways. We have expanded on a few of them in this book. If you want to identify your talents and use them to your advantage, then peruse the coming sections. In the coming section, we have tried to answer the most sought-after question – "How to discover your talent," in the coming section.

Discover your talents using the following steps:

1. Examine your life.
Every life assessment is unique from the others. Each Life Assessment examination would be unique from the others. Take this assessment to find out more about your potential in life. In addition to being cost-free, it gives you insight into your performance in all spheres of life. You'll be able to recognize and focus on the aspect of life that requires the most care.

Additionally, with the help of such tests, you can realize what makes you tick.

The Myers-Briggs Type Indicator is one of the most promising tools that can help you define your life and personality patterns. It would allow you to check what types of motivations in life are more suited to you.

Once you can judge the category you come into, you can list your strengths and shortcomings more precisely.

You can even use the results of such tests for a walk-in interview, on a date, or any other high-stakes situation. Play around with your newly discovered strengths.

2. Identify your sources of strength. The key to discovering your talent is realizing what makes you stronger. Stronger means that you have to have a purpose in life and grow and be satisfied with who you are. That is the main purpose of this life. You have probably seen circumstances in which everything appears perfect and simple.

It seems easier to do everything when you are good at something. We are naturally drawn to things that provide us with inner peace and contentment.

However, you feel low when you feel out of place or do not get that satisfaction from your daily life.

These are the times to identify and recall what made you feel good about your life. It might be your talent to deal with kids or play games.

Whatever it may be, that would define your strength matter what you are good at, you must make sure to pursue such talents. If you have a lot of experience with children, consider volunteering at an after-school program or babysitting. That's what would allow you to tailor your schedule to your advantage.

3. Determine your biggest spending area. Examining your most frequent spending areas is one of the finest methods to spot talent. If you struggle to keep accurate books or financial records, you might want to consider utilizing simple, free apps like Mint. It would enable you to ascertain the expenditure of your maximum amount of money. You would find your gift if you followed your green. Examining your

money over the last year will reveal a definite spending trend on particular items. Should you regularly shell out cash to maintain your fitness regimen, perhaps your skill is in it! Take advantage of this talent discovery by progressing through these activities to the next level and living life to the fullest. You would be quite satisfied with this.

4. Find out from your friends what they think best and worst about you. Instead, why not respond by reaching out to your closest friends and family members? Since they have known you for a long time, they are the ones who are most likely to be well aware of your interests and hobbies. Above all, they can identify your strengths.

Anything from dancing to singing to telling jokes can be done. Your abilities are those things that come naturally to you and make other people smile.
When you ask your friends about your best and worst qualities, ask them to be brutally honest

with you. Knowing about your weaknesses or worst qualities helps you isolate such habits or activities from your life. This would only leave you with things that you are good at.

5. Ask your family what you loved as a child. Why not talk to your mother, dad, or siblings and check with them about what you loved when you were a child?
Maybe you are having difficulty remembering such things, but they will surely remember. These are the people in your life who have known you for the longest.

There are things and habits that we pick up as kids and try to be good at these. Maybe we were good at it, but we tended to forget such things as we grew up.
Your past behaviors, likes, and dislikes would give you a clear insight into your personality and how you grew up.
If some of these things still tickle your brain or bring excitement, these were the things that you loved and were good at. That's what your

talent is! Try to recreate your childhood and bring back the same level of gusto when you realize your strengths.

6.Write in a journal.
Sometimes nothing works, and we just don't feel like discussing our feelings with anyone. Do you know what is good during such times? Using a pen and paper would be the best companion when you need to be alone and discover your talents.

Take your journal and let your thoughts go wild. Write something every day in this journal and make it your routine activity. When you allow your thoughts to flow freely, they will direct you to the things you love.
After about a week or a month, start re-reading your journal. You will realize that numerous things would attract your attention, and you would like to revisit those thoughts.

Your journal holds the answer to discovering your talents. It would show you what you miss from your life and what you need to do next. It would also allow you to discover what you desire.

Reading your journal will allow you to list down your strengths and opportunities.

7. Look for talent in others.

Don't force yourself to do so when you cannot dig deep down in your mindset. Take a break and observe others. There are times when the talent of others inspires us. What attracts us could secretly become our talent.

Sometimes observing others also inspires us to realize that we are good at it. For example, if an article inspires you but you believe you could have contributed to it in a better way, maybe your hidden talent is writing.

Look out for something that connects to your soul. It should inspire you and make you feel happy and content.

There would be times when the talent of others would make you feel jealous. But worry not, you can use this to your advantage too! You can seek advice from such a person and get help to develop such talent yourself.

8. Take stock of your book/music/movie collections.
We live in a modern society full of audio and video content everywhere. If you collect books, music, or movies, this would be a good time to check your inventory.

Try to mind what type of media you consume. The category of media that you are fond of reflects your clear inclination to enjoy it. Sometimes that helps us determine our identity. Some things light a fire in our lives.

Our media collection would give us an idea of what we like. If you find a specific pattern towards a particular segment, dig deep into it by finding other related activities.
Connect with others who follow similar talents. Sometimes even they can guide us through the next steps of discovering the hidden talents.

9. Remember what you have been thanked for.
We do numerous deeds in our lifetime. For a few, we are thanked, and for others, we are not. Try to find out the various things you were thanked for in the past. How did it make you feel?

If you feel good, then try to recollect if doing a similar errand at a later stage also leads to getting "thanks" from someone. When you are thanked for something regularly, you are good at it, which could be your hidden talent.

You might be a good listener, a good motivator, or a good teacher. These small thank yous may seem insignificant at times. However, somewhere deep down, these are our talents.

10. Be open to change.
Once you have found how to identify talent, be open to change. You might have to make major life-changing decisions after discovering your talent.

It might seem unsettling initially, but that is what will make you happy eventually. You cannot expect to stay stagnant and grow. You need to accept change and do it willingly. Don't retort to finding reasons to delay or neglect such changes. You need to give yourself a chance to live a life that makes you happy through your talents.

You will have to let go of all the preconceived notions and willingly accept the new thoughts and habits. You will find that such changes would make you content and prepare you for more life challenges.

11. Select Your Talents
It might turn out that you are multi-talented. You can be good with more than one thing in life. And this can be a good thing since it proves to be very motivating.
You need to choose from the list of things you are good at during such times.

Decide what talent ticks your heart and soul. What makes you happy and content is what you should shortlist and pursue.

Just choose and dig deep into your passions to live a happy and content life.

12. Upgrade

Discovering your talent does not mean that your story of self-discovery has ended. It requires you to constantly learn and upgrade your knowledge and become more proficient to upgrade your skills.

Take up courses, attend seminars, watch videos, read books, or do anything that will help you with upgrading your talent.
With time almost everything becomes outdated, and therefore you should never be satisfied when it comes to learning and upgrading your knowledge.

13. Reach Perfection

Perfection is constant evolution and up-gradation of knowledge. Flawlessness means to become better compared to the person you were yesterday!

Hustle, question constantly, select your abilities, update, and arrive at your compulsiveness. Be the best form of you! That is how you reach perfection!

Final Thoughts
Life is not always a straight line. It is sometimes zigzag or runs in circles. We need to be aware of our strengths if we need to deal with the ups and downs of our lives. Our strengths give us the courage and vision to fight mental demons and face life's challenges. Let the above pointers guide you to discover your talents

Chapter 3

Identifying your passion

Remember back when you were a kid? You would just do things. You never thought to yourself, "What are the relative merits of learning baseball versus football?" You just ran around the playground and played baseball and football. You built sand castles and played tag and asked silly questions and looked for bugs and dug up grass and pretended you were a sewer monster.

Nobody told you to do it, you just did it. You were led merely by your curiosity and excitement.
And the beautiful thing was, if you hated baseball, you just stopped playing it. There was no guilt involved. There was no arguing or debate. You either liked it or you didn't.
And if you loved looking for bugs, you just did that. There was no second-level analysis of,

"Well, is looking for bugs really what I should be doing with my time as a child? Nobody else wants to look for bugs, does that mean there's something *wrong with me*? How will looking for bugs affect my prospects?"

There was no bullshit. If you liked something, you just did it.

"HOW DO I FIND MY PASSION?"

Today, I received approximately the 11,504th email this year from a person telling me that they don't know *what to do with their life*. And like all of the others, this person asked me if I had any ideas of what they could do, *where they could start*, where to "find their passion."

And of course, I didn't respond. Why? Because I have no fucking clue. If you don't have any idea what to do with yourself, what makes you think some jackass with a website would? I'm a writer, not a fortune teller.

But more importantly, what I want to say to these people is this: that's the whole point—" not knowing" is the whole fucking point. Life is all about *not knowing*, and then doing something anyway.

All of life is like this. All of it. And it's not going to get any easier just because you found out you love your job cleaning septic tanks, or you scored a dream gig writing indie movies.

The common complaint among a lot of these people is that they need to "find their passion."

I call bullshit. You already found your passion, you're just ignoring it. Seriously, you're awake 16 hours a day, what the fuck do you do with your time? You're doing something. You're talking about something. There's some topic activity or idea that dominates a significant amount of your free time, your conversations, and your web browsing, and it dominates them without you consciously pursuing it or looking for it.

It's right there in front of you, you're just avoiding it. For whatever reason, you're avoiding it. You're telling yourself, "Oh well, yeah, I love comic books but that doesn't count. You can't make money with comic books."

Fuck you, have you even tried?

The problem is not a lack of passion for something. The problem is *productivity*. The problem is *perception*. The problem is *acceptance*.

The problem is, "Oh, well that's just not a realistic option," or "Mom and Dad would kill me if I tried to do that, they say I should be a doctor," or "That's crazy, you can't buy a BMW with the money you make doing that."

The problem isn't passion. It's never a passion. It's priorities.

And even then, who says you need to make money *doing what you love*? Since when does everyone feel entitled to love every fucking second of their job?

Really, what is so wrong with working an okay, normal job with some cool people you like and then pursuing your passion in your free time on the side? Has the world turned upside-down or is this suddenly a novel idea to people?

Look, here's another slap in the face for you: every job sucks sometimes. There's no such thing as some passionate activity that you will never get tired of, never get stressed over, never complain about.

It doesn't exist. I am living my *dream job* (which happened by accident, by the way. I never in a million years planned on this happening; like a kid on a playground I just went and tried it), and I still hate about 30% of it. Some days more.
Again, that's just life.
The issue here is, once again, *expectations*. If you think you're supposed to be working 70-hour work weeks and sleeping in your office like Steve Jobs and loving every second of it, you've been watching too many shitty movies.

If you think you're supposed to wake up every single day dancing out of your pajamas because you get to go to work, then you've been drinking the Kool-Aid. Life doesn't work like that. It's just *unrealistic*. There's a thing most of us need called *balance*.

"Just follow your passion!" You've heard it before and you'll hear it again from well-meaning family members, guidance counselors, Disney movies, and online motivational speakers with volume control issues. And yeah, sure, you'd love to follow this advice—if only you knew what your passion was.

If you're feeling stuck, here are six steps to discover what you want to do with your life. Take time to work through the process and know that, no matter what, you'll be getting closer to where you want to be.

1. Start with the right perspective.

If you go into a restaurant thinking, "I'm not hungry. There'll be nothing here I want to eat. I don't want to be here," the menu isn't going to look appealing. You won't give it your time or attention, and you're unlikely to find food you'll enjoy.

The same principle applies to passion-seeking. If you're convinced that finding your passion is hard, or that it's not going to happen for you, you'll remain closed to possibilities. You'll block the little nudges, pulls, and signals that guide us. After all, how can you expect to find fulfilling work if you don't believe it exists?

Instead, choose to adopt the perspective that you *can* do what you love with your life and you *will* find your passion. One of the best ways to strengthen this point of view is to surround yourself with and talk to people who are living examples.

If you have friends and family who are following their passions, have a conversation with them about how they found what they loved and began to work toward making it their career or a significant part of their lives. It might also be a good time to expand your circle; and associate with—and be inspired by—people who love their work. You can start on LinkedIn or with alumni groups—reach out to the people who seem to be following their passion and set up a few informational interviews.

2. Think about what you've already enjoyed doing.
Once you've decided that your passion is findable, it's time to look for evidence of what you already love to do. If you scan the landscape of your life, you'll notice certain experiences peak up above the horizon. It's so valuable to delve into these "peak moments" and extract the key ingredients.

Consider yourself a beach trawler, discerning between the gold and the cheap metal. For example, one of my favorite summer jobs involved teaching English to teenagers. I might assume the key ingredient was the English language or young people.

But when I paid attention to my metaphorical metal detector, it became clear that the bleep went off when I was being a leader within a community and teaching that community something of great value to them. That's exactly what I do now in my work—but without the teenagers, present perfect tense, or vocabulary tests!

So think of all the experiences you've had that you've loved most—without limiting yourself just to work experiences—and investigate what made them so fulfilling.

If there was a job you loved, what were your tasks? What kind of work environment was it? What was the company working toward? Who did you get to interact with? What was most exciting and/or satisfying? Or maybe you still reminisce about the trip you took to Europe after college.

Did you love it because you saw new things and learned about new cultures? Or because of the people you were with? Or maybe it was the problem-solving you had to do to make it from one country to the other on the small number of Euros you had budgeted?

Look for themes that come up a lot or that you feel strongly about. These are your key ingredients.

3. Explore ways to tie the things you like together.
When you look at all the ingredients that matter to you, they might at first seem entirely disconnected. Let's say you love speaking French, playing with words, analyzing and categorizing, and being a leader within a community.

How could you construct a career from these? It'd be like peering into your *Chopped* basket and seeing cocoa powder, tofu, and carrots and wondering: How could I possibly make something delicious that includes all of these?

This is the time to look beyond the ingredients and choose a meal; something that all of these ingredients can come together to make. For example, my colleague Abby—whose diverse passions are described above—helps business owners find the right words to fit their brands. She analyzes and categorizes copy into what she calls "voice values." She draws wisdom from previously running a funky French lifestyle boutique, and French words pepper her copy, giving her brand that special *je ne sais quoi.*

What kind of career would allow you to incorporate as many of your ingredients as you can? Take into account not just job duties, but work environments, company goals and missions, and even how this career would fit into the life you want outside of work.

4. Discern between a hobby and a profitable passion.

It might be that, through this exploration, you fall head over heels in love with an activity that engrosses you—something that lights you up and makes your heart sing. But now you have to ask yourself the next question: Who would benefit from (and pay for) this?

Well, if you want to contribute your passion to society and make an income from it, you need to get realistic about whether this could turn into a career—and what you would need to do to make that happen.

For example, my client Lisa loves to draw. She makes art for the sheer joy of it. When she attempted to turn this profitable business, she realized that the market that was hungriest for her talents was business owners who needed illustrations for their blogs, websites, and products. This felt like play to Lisa, but to make her services marketable, she also needed to add tech skills to her toolkit, so that her design work could be usable online by her ideal clients.

So do your research. This is another step where networking and informational interviews are your friends. Talk to people who are following the same passion and find out if they're making a living off of it, how, and what other skills and work go into making your passion profitable.

There are also plenty of free online resources that can point you toward a plausible career that builds on particular interests. For example, if your passions involve writing and reading, you can check out our list of jobs for people who love words.

You should also think about whether you would *enjoy* doing these things for a living; for some people, a passion is just fun, and turning it into work changes it from a "love to do" to a "have to do" they're no longer excited about.

5. Break down your fears—so you can overcome them.

When you seek your passion, there will be parts of you that go into rebellion. I'd guess that this article itself might be provoking some of those resistant parts! We all have a huge number of fears—around failure, success, visibility, and vulnerability—that speak in sensible voices, instructing us that we mustn't do what we love. If you let these voices win, your passion will remain out of your grasp. Instead, look for the fear beneath each supposedly reasonable voice. Uncover the years of conditioning—from parents, school, partners, and colleagues—and reassure the remaining parts that your ship is sailing in the right direction. In other words, figure out why you might be resisting following your passion and what you need to do to assuage your fears.

For example, if you're afraid of not having enough money to get by, you might consider saving up before you make any big moves, or starting to pursue your passion on the side while working a full-time job. If you're convinced you're not good enough to succeed doing what you're passionate about, break down why you think that and if these fears are ultimately unfounded or if they stem from wanting to hone certain skills or learn more.

6. Find *your* right next step.
On my journey, I've mostly lived by the motto: "Leap and the net will appear." I've noticed I couldn't find the news until I'd said farewell to

the old. With each step into the unknown—for example, giving my notice at my part-time salaried job to go fully self-employed—my announcement to the universe has been: "I'm available. I'm serious about this." But that doesn't need to be your method.

Find your version of brave. Discover what risks work for you. Maybe you don't have the option to leave your job without a guaranteed income, but maybe you can enroll in a class connected to your passion or look for a new job that helps you gain a skill you'll need to reach your goal.

The path of passion is where you do things that scare you enough, without leaving you in a constant state of fear. Expand your comfort zone, rather than leaving it.

Chapter 4

Focus your talent

If you want to succeed in life, you must focus on what you can do, not on what you cannot do.
Focus can bring tremendous power to your work, passion, and vocation. Without focus, you will never accomplish much. With focus, you find that your talents quadruple; they gain direction and power. And those qualities produce results.

One, like initiative, the focus is cultivated; it does not come naturally to most people. We are glued to a culture with infinite choices. Thus, we find ourselves pulled in scores of directions.

A cultivated, deepened, and enlarged talent is worth more than a thousand shallow faculties. The first law of success is concentration- to bend all your energies in one direction, going to that one point, looking neither to the right nor to the left.

Two, focus increases your energy. When you aspire to reach a goal, you will first find your target. If you lack focus, you will attempt everything at once. That will sap your energy and rob you of new opportunities.

In contrast, focus energizes your passion. Few men, during their lifetime, come anywhere near exhausting the resources dwelling within them. There are deep wells of strength that are never used.

One reason those wells often go untapped is lack of focus. Something wonderful happens when we narrow our focus on set goals. That is the magic.

The mind does not reach toward achievement until it has a clear objective.

Three, focus lifts you; it enables you to eclipse your contemporaries to a degree that it will astonish your relations.

In a sea of mediocrity, just knowing what you want and pursuing it distinguishes you from everyone else.

One great American writer, Henry David Thoreau, asked: "Did you ever hear of a man who had striven all his life faithfully and singly towards an object and in no measure obtained it? If a man constantly aspires, is he not elevated?"

Focus always has an impact. Just by striving to be better than you are, you become elevated, even if you don't accomplish what you desire and even if others don't step aside for you. You cannot shoot for the stars and remain unaffected by the effort.

Fourth, the focus expands your life. When we focus our attention on the subject at hand, we can expand ideas in a way that we wouldn't be able to do otherwise.

Thus, what you focus on expands. Narrowing your view widens your perspective.

Five, the focus must be intentionally sustained. People do not naturally remain focused; it takes a lot of effort to remain focused. What separates the champion from the mediocre is that he concentrates just a little longer. Several years ago, I memorized a definition of success to help me in my career. "Success is the progressive realization of a predetermined goal."

What I learned from that definition is that success isn't an event; it is a process. And anytime you engage in a process that takes time, you must remain focused. Only focused people can direct their talent to achieve success.

For you to become a genius, you must make every action count towards a focused goal. You will have removed most of the roadblocks to success when you know the difference between motion and direction. People who are undecided about what they want cannot tap into their strength of will or talent. As a result, they will only drift into mediocrity.

To succeed in life, effort and courage are not enough; you must have purpose and direction.

Do not allow your yesterday to hijack your today. There has never been a person who focused on his past that had a better future. Instead, they should learn from the past and forget it.

A retentive memory might be a good thing, but the ability to forget is the true token of greatness. Champions know the past is irrevocable.

Life is a race, so you cannot afford to look back. Your eye is on the finish line. If you desire to achieve success, you must make what you are doing now your focus.

Six, focus on the present. If you are always thinking of tomorrow, you will never get anything done today. Your focus must remain where you have control- today. If you focus on today, you will get a better tomorrow.

Today's lessons become tomorrow's books.
Stay focused on results. By focusing on results,
you stay positive and encouraged.

Chapter5

Follow Your Passions and Success Will Follow
Whether you are considering starting a small business or changing career paths, factoring passion into your decisions can lead to more success.

Characteristics such as strong values, talent, ambition, intellect, discipline, persistence, and luck all contribute to business and career success. However, you may find that following your passion may make the most significant difference of all. Let's look at some examples of successful entrepreneurs who have followed a career path doing what they love.

KEY TAKEAWAYS

-Whether you are starting a small business or changing career paths, factor passion for your work into the equation.

-Success can also come from strong values, talent, intellect, persistence, and luck.

-Steve Jobs believed in the power of passion and claimed that his passion for his work made all the difference.

-Warren Buffett, known as "the Oracle of Omaha" and one of the most widely known investors, has said that there is more to success than money.

Meaning of Success
Before discussing passion and explaining its significance, you may want to reflect on what success means. Success is usually thought of as making large sums of wealth or achieving a certain level of fame, but many people define success in life in a way that is not all about money.

Success can be defined as the achievement of a desired aim or purpose. More than money or fame, most people desire to align their passions with their work while making a sustainable income.

For many people, success means being proud of achievements and being part of something that makes a difference. This is particularly true when it comes to meaningful work.

If you follow your passion, you are more likely to put more time and effort into your work, which can lead to more success.

Why Passion Is So Important?

If enthusiasm and passion are present, people tend to be more resilient when encountering obstacles. People who are passionate about what they do, rather than just working for the money alone tend to have more positive outlooks that can help them overcome difficulty through problem-solving.

Also, if you are more passionate about your job, you may be more inclined to work hard on self-improvement and broadening your skill set, which will increase your chances of success.

4 Cases of Success from Passion for Work

Steve Jobs
One of the most successful companies in the world is Apple. Apple's founder and most notable leader was the late Steve Jobs. In a Forbes article titled "The Seven Success Principles of Steve Jobs," writer Carmine Gallo outlines seven factors responsible for Jobs' success. The article is based on interviews with Apple employees and Steve Jobs himself. The first principle? "Do what you love."[1]
Steve Jobs believed in the power of passion and once said, "People with passion can change the world for the better."[2] Jobs claimed that his passion for his work made all the difference.

Chris Gardner
Chris Gardner was once homeless but became a multi-millionaire stockbroker. He was featured

in the movie *The Pursuit of Happiness,* and he expressed what he believes is the secret to success. According to Gardner, the secret is to "find something you love to do so much you can't wait for the sun to rise to do it all over again."3 He explains that the most inspiring leaders do not simply work but pursue a calling.

Mark Zuckerberg
Mark Zuckerberg, CEO of Meta (formerly Facebook), has changed the world in which we live with his social media platform. In David Kirkpatrick's book *The Facebook Effect: The Inside Story of the Company That is Connecting The World,* Kirkpatrick lists what he believes are Zuckerberg's characteristics that led to his success.4

One of these characteristics is following his passion, not money. Zuckerberg suggests "following your happiness" when at a crossroads, using the logic that even if you do not end up making a fortune, you will at least be doing what you love.

Warren Buffett
Warren Buffett, known as "the Oracle of Omaha," is probably one of the greatest investors of all time. But even Buffett said there is more to success than money. In an interview with *Parade Magazine,* Buffett outlined 10 ways to get rich.

He concluded his list of advice with, "Know what success means."5 He explains the importance of finding what brings true meaning and what makes each day meaningful, which should be the focus of an individual's efforts.

Changing Jobs
Many people are dissatisfied with their jobs. However, the need for healthcare and a steady income are reasons that you may feel compelled to stay in your position.

However, if there is a way for you to navigate the financial hurdles and pursue your passion in a niche area, hard work and success might come easier. Enjoying the work you do can be more important to fostering happiness than having a large bank account.

How Do I Know It's Time to Change Jobs?

There are several signs it may be time for you to change jobs. If you are dreading work and feel like you no longer care about the quality of your work, it may be time to change jobs. If you feel unsafe or bullied at work, you may also want to look for another job. Finally, if you cannot advance in your career with new challenges and higher pay, you may want to find an opportunity in another job.

What Are the Disadvantages of Switching Jobs?

When you change jobs for a better opportunity, you may face a few downsides as well. For example, you may have to change health insurance policies and shift the funds in your

401(k) plan to a new employer. You'll also have to start fresh with making workplace connections with your colleagues.

What Should You Never Reveal in a Job Interview?

If you are changing jobs, you will likely undergo an interview before you are hired into a new position. Some things you should never reveal in a job interview include too much personal information, negative feelings about past employers, and your unresolved weaknesses.

The Bottom Line

Your decision about your work and your career will be based on several factors that are unique to your situation, including your financial needs and your goals. However, including your passion for your work in your decision-making can lead you on a career path you enjoy that will encourage you to dedicate your time and effort, which can lead to success

Chapter 6

Energized with confidence

In the workplace, confidence matters as much as ability—the higher the confidence, the higher the performance. Confidence is the foundation for becoming a strong leader, pursuing challenges, taking risks and putting one's self in positions to learn and grow.

Lack of confidence drives risk aversion and makes employees less willing to pursue challenges. Businesses lose out on innovation, productivity and strong leadership, while individuals miss out on opportunity, career advancement and personal development.

Lack of confidence not only holds women back, it holds companies back. According to one of the most comprehensive business case studies ever conducted, companies that perform best financially have the greatest numbers of women in leadership roles.

[i] Yet statistics suggest that lack of confidence is holding women back from leadership opportunities. While more than 50 percent of women hold college degrees
[ii] and close to 40 percent have MBAs
[iii], they comprise less than 5 percent of Fortune 500 CEO positions
[iv] and only about 15 percent of senior executive positions.
[v]Improved confidence allows women to step into and excel in these roles.

While there is no shortage of information around The Confidence Gap in the workplace, there is shockingly little on what to DO about it. That is why this program is essential.
Building confidence in one aspect of our lives transfers to all of them. Training in the following areas creates confidence and competence that can be applied to one's professional life.

-Confidence is influenced by how well we know our values and purpose. When we lack clarity, we typically lack confidence as well. It is difficult to feel confident in our abilities when we are uncertain about why and how we make decisions.

But once we truly understand ourselves, then our decisions will naturally align with our ideals. We will grow in confidence as we learn to trust our internal locus rather than be swayed by external forces.

-Confidence is shaped by what we consume.

What we watch, listen to and read can make us feel either positive and empowered or inadequate and insecure. Unfortunately, much of the information we "eat" is junk, filling us with empty "calories" and making us weak. In order to nurture confidence, we must nurture our minds with nourishing input.

-Confidence is affected by recovery. Our days are filled with incessant obligations and habitual time wasters. How can we feel confident when it seems we are not doing enough or not doing it well enough? Recovery means granting ourselves permission to refuel and recharge. Only then will there be time and space for confidence to grow.

-Confidence is linked to our physical being. In particular, we can use movement in strategic ways to connect and change.

Our movement needs vary from day to day and person to person. Gentle forms of movement help us center and connect to the inner power within us. More challenging types of movement allow us to build grit and tenacity—if it doesn't challenge us, it doesn't change us.

Confidence comes from taking action. This interactive and engaging program teaches women how to develop daily practices that embolden confidence and competence in the workplace and beyond, thus helping companies to have their female employees unleash their untapped potential.

Rich with discussion and inner reflection, this course utilizes the wisdom and experiences of the entire group. Attendees leave with personalized plans for taking action in the interrelated areas of inner reflection, thoughtful consumption, strategic movement and regular recovery

Do you find yourself lacking confidence each time you make a decision?

Are you constantly living in fear of the unknown, which makes you doubt the feasibility and possibilities of your decisions?

Whether it's career decisions, family decisions, financial decisions, marriage decisions, or general life decisions, the first step to achieving success in your decisions is trusting and being confident about them.

Ever wondered how much time people spend worrying about the choices they make in their personal and professional lives? Surveys show a substantial amount of time, as daily stress continues to reach record highs, with more Americans reporting they are suffering from anxiety as a response to stress over any other reaction.

Award-winning speaker and Energy Leadership Index™ Master Practitioner, Rebecca Ahmed, will share how you can energize your values to confidently make decisions that align with your vision and mission.

Rebecca will break down limiting beliefs and educate the audience on creating values-driven solutions for any challenge that comes their way. She will share case studies on how to align one's values with their choices, repurposing wasted energy previously spent on worrying, and energizing action steps towards their goal(s).

Key Takeaways:
-Discover three easy steps for identifying and defining your values and motivators.
-Recognize limiting beliefs currently holding you back from confidently making decisions that support your goals and mission.

-Understand how to customize energetic principles to create action plans to achieve your specific objectives.

-Strategically align your values to your solutions to make confident decisions that immediately and permanently increase your energy and reduce your anxiety.

Audience members will identify their values and motivators using the three simple steps Rebecca will unveil. She will be there to offer guidance at every step and help you internalize the technique as you progress.

Once you recognize your values and motivators, you can easily align them to your solutions and balloon your energy levels. With greater energy comes clarity and determination, two core elements for making confident decisions and eliminating unhealthy beliefs

Chapter 7

Multiply your success: The power of teamwork

We know teamwork is important, but how important?
Being a master of one or a jack-of-all-trades in today's world does not bring about success if you are unable to work as part of a team. The importance of teamwork cannot be stressed enough.

In the current economy, most of our jobs involve interacting with others, so, being able to perform well with your colleagues is key to attaining growth and success. In every aspect of our business at Yale, the diverse skills of our teams are needed to achieve success. Teamwork is an essential skill to help us accomplish our organizational goals and objectives.

Here are 5 reasons why teamwork is important and why it matters to you:

1.Teamwork benefits from differing perspectives and feedback.

2. A team environment allows individuals to bring their diverse perspectives to problem-solving, which in turn increases their success at arriving at solutions more efficiently and effectively.

The contributions of everyone are more valued when solicited in team meetings. The improvement in "Group IQ" is gratifying and shows up in decisions affecting the team. When all members of a team operate without undue hierarchy and encourage everyone's feedback, people tend to be more open about their ideas.

If you feel a sense of safe connection with your teammates, you will be more likely to confidently share your opinions and thoughts without fear of judgment, even when views disagree. Research suggests that such a climate of "psychological safety" in teams results in more engagement, creativity, and innovation.

3. Teamwork leads to learning.

4. Individuals have their own set of skills and strengths. When the whole team works as a unit, everyone has an opportunity to learn from each other. This process leads to resource building and enables the team to become better equipped to deal with new challenges.

5. Teamwork can improve efficiency and productivity.

6. One person working on a project is always going to take longer to complete it in comparison to the collaborative efforts of many.

Efficiency rules when work is appropriately divided within a team, responsibilities are shared, and tasks are more likely to be finished within a set time frame. Good teamwork also enhances group outcomes and the measurable effectiveness of organizations.

7. Teamwork cultivates communication and strong work relationships.

8. Teamwork can be effective in building great work relationships. We do not mean that team members must be the best of friends. Rather, a great working relationship flows from the right frame of mind where you collaborate with positive intent, respect, and active listening.

Great team communication is founded on a desire for mutual understanding and trust. When working together on a common goal or deliverable as an integrated whole, individual members consistently encourage and support each other.

Indeed, one of the most prized benefits of good teamwork is a reduction in perceived work stress. Camaraderie and a sense of friendship among team members are associated with the highest levels of morale and job satisfaction.

1. Teamwork brings an expanded sense of accomplishment.
2. When a team works on a project as one unit, the sense of accomplishment we experience expands beyond our achievements.

Teamwork can fulfill the human desire for belonging and contributing to something greater than ourselves. This is yet another reason why developing teamwork skills is worth everyone's investment.
Teamwork divides the task and multiplies the success.
In the pursuit of success, individuals often find themselves facing daunting challenges and overwhelming responsibilities.

At the heart of the statement lies the idea of dividing tasks among team members. When a group comes together to work on a common objective, the workload is distributed among individuals based on their strengths, expertise, and capabilities.

This division of labor allows each team member to focus on specific aspects of the project, leveraging their skills and knowledge to the fullest.

Teamwork fosters efficiency and productivity in multiple ways.

- First, it reduces the risk of burnout. When tasks are shared, individuals can work with more enthusiasm and energy, as they are not overwhelmed by an excessive workload.
- Second, it promotes specialization. Team members can hone their skills in specific areas, leading to higher-quality work.

- Third, collaboration leads to better problem-solving. Diverse perspectives and experiences contribute to innovative solutions that may not have emerged from individual efforts.

Teamwork doesn't just divide tasks; it also multiplies creativity and innovation. When people with different backgrounds, experiences, and viewpoints collaborate, they bring a diverse set of ideas to the table. This diversity sparks creativity as team members brainstorm, challenge each other's assumptions, and explore new possibilities. The synergy created through collaboration often results in breakthrough solutions that propel the team toward success.

Another critical aspect of teamwork is the support and motivation it provides. Team members can encourage and uplift each other during challenging times. When someone faces a setback, the team rallies to offer solutions and emotional support.

This collective encouragement helps individuals persevere and stay motivated. Knowing that their efforts contribute to the team's success can be a powerful motivator for each member.

Teamwork also serves as a risk mitigation strategy. In projects with complex challenges or uncertainties, having a team allows for a more comprehensive risk assessment. Team members can identify potential pitfalls, develop contingency plans, and react swiftly to unforeseen issues.

Teamwork isn't just about accomplishing tasks; it's about achieving remarkable success that surpasses what any individual could accomplish alone.

Chapter 8

Guiding Others to their Success Intersection.

Effective onboarding of new employees is crucial for organizations to maintain productivity and achieve long-term success.

Managers play a pivotal role in this process, with their ability to set up new hires for success being paramount. By establishing well-defined objectives, managers can empower new employees, enhance their confidence and propel them toward growth and achievement in their new positions.

Below, 20 Business Council members share their best tips, tricks and tools for managers to ensure new employees thrive and make meaningful contributions from day one.

-Pair New Team Members With A Mentor

At our company, every new team member is paired with a mentor on a cross-departmental team who embodies our values and lives our ethos of "finding a better way." By creating personalized learning plans and promoting a sense of community, new employees understand that they're integral to our shared vision, not just filling a job slot.

-Clearly Communicate During Onboarding

Onboarding is everything. Clearly communicate expectations, provide relevant training resources and foster a supportive environment for feedback and questions. Also, regular check-ins during the initial onboarding period can help managers identify any difficulties and offer timely solutions.

-Be Vulnerable

Vulnerability, especially from a leader, facilitates authentic team communication, which cultivates an understanding, supportive environment. I intentionally make an effort to be vulnerable in front of my team to show them we are in a safe space. When people feel that they can be vulnerable, they will more readily share the areas in which they need help and support, making all employees, both new and old, successful.

-Ask How You Can Best Provide Feedback

One of my favorite things to ask a new employee that I manage is, "How can I best provide you with feedback?" It shows the employee that you, as a manager, care about providing feedback, are cognizant of different communication styles and value them as a partner in work. If every new manager could learn to ask this question, it would set up all their employees for success.

-Motivate With A Worthwhile Goal

More than anything, people are motivated by a worthwhile goal. So, as early as possible, help new employees fall in love with a customer problem, as it will connect them to the reason your company exists and give them a sense of ownership. Doing this will start them off on the right foot and show them that their work really matters in the real world.

-Establish Trust And High Autonomy

Top talent expects workplace cultures with high trust and high autonomy. The hiring process is when candidates earn trust; what they lack on day one is domain expertise or the ins and outs of the company. Managers can facilitate introductory meetings between new hires and key players to help new team members integrate quickly.

-Create A Support Structure Team

Ahead of their start date, create a string and structure of support for each new hire's first three months. From their point-person(s) in HR and the "work-buddy" who holds their hand for the first few days to the team member helping train and settle them in, everyone in the line of support must be available and affable! A new employee's first few months go a long way in helping them to form the bond and adaptability needed for their success on the job.

-Communicate The Significance Of The Role

Communicating role significance to new employees fosters a sense of purpose and belonging, which is crucial for engagement and motivation. Understanding their contribution to team performance, company growth and customer satisfaction helps employees see the broader impact of their work. Additionally, it fuels passion, encourages proactive participation and stimulates innovation.

-Maintain A Strong Work Ethic And Goal Orientation

Having a strong work ethic is crucial in any new business position. It means being dedicated to putting in the necessary effort and being willing to go the extra mile to achieve goals. It also means being goal-oriented, which helps in defining clear objectives and then working toward them. Set realistic targets, create action plans and consistently track the progress.

-Open Meetings With Personal Connections

With remote companies, it can be difficult to assimilate and build personal connections that help you achieve success. If new hires are on board remotely, a practical tip is to open meetings by offering something new and personal about yourself as well as trying to get to know something new about your colleagues. Doing this will help forge more human, authentic connections between you and your colleagues.

-Become Your Employees' Biggest Supporter

Empower employees to be incredible. Become their cheerleader, their defensive formation and their accelerant. Make them believe that everything is possible and do everything in your power to make that a reality.

-Provide Resources And Learning Materials

When an employee arrives at a new position, it is always helpful for them to read literature relevant to the new responsibilities they are meant to handle. They can also benefit from reaching out to people who have already achieved success in similar positions and asking for their insights. A manager's job in this case would be to ensure that these new employees have access to such tools.

-Put The Company Vision Front And Center

Companies that stand the test of time all have something in common: A clear and simple vision. The first and most important goal is to make sure the company vision is front and center in the workplace, well understood and an integral part of the team's daily experience. Managers need to help employees connect the dots so that they can strongly align with the company's values and mission.

-Provide Product Training

It's essential for new employees to focus on getting to know your product first. Allocate the first few days specifically for training. This training should cover in-depth information about the product, its features, functionalities and any other relevant details. By the end of the training, conduct a mandatory assessment to evaluate the employee's understanding and knowledge of the product.

-Embrace Their Individuality

Embrace your new hires' individuality. Understand their interests and capabilities. Invest time in getting to know each new member of your diverse workforce. Avoid forcing people into predefined ways of getting results. Instead, use what you learn about them to mold the job to their strengths, keeping in mind that different paths can yield equal or superior results.

-Have An Open-Door Policy

Have a manager-inspired open-door policy. All positions in a company have burnout points, and most of the time, new employees do not know where they are or when they show up.

Managers can clearly outline where and when employees in the past have experienced burnout and be committed to being totally hands-on during and after those challenges.

-Create A Comprehensive Onboarding Experience

Invest in comprehensive onboarding. Set clear expectations, provide thorough training and assign a mentor. Encourage open communication and create a welcoming environment. By nurturing their growth, you foster confidence and productivity, ensuring new employees integrate smoothly and thrive in their new roles.

-Provide Resources And Incentives

Understand what your new employee's values are so that you can align incentives and motivate them. Provide resources and guides to help the employee succeed.

If you do not have all the protocol, guidance and training material ready to set expectations, then make sure your management style and the employee's work ethics are aligned. Remote versus in-person work settings will also impact your approach.

-Ask Employees To Repeat Responsibilities Back To You

After managers explain and onboard their new positions, then ask your new employees to take you back through what their roles and responsibilities are. Many times, managers believe they've explained it clearly, but your employees may have heard things differently.

-Foster Transparent Communication And Confidence

Carve the path of success for your new team members by establishing transparency and clarity in your communication. Enlighten them about their roles, plant the seeds of expectation and cultivate an atmosphere of trust and confidence where questions are welcomed. Encourage them to innovate, share suggestions and learn from mistakes.